my first animal

LETTER TRACING & COLORING BOOK

- for preschoolers -

Let's get started by practicing straight
lines and curves.

After finishing the whole book, come
back to the beginning and write down
the animal names.

Trace the straight lines

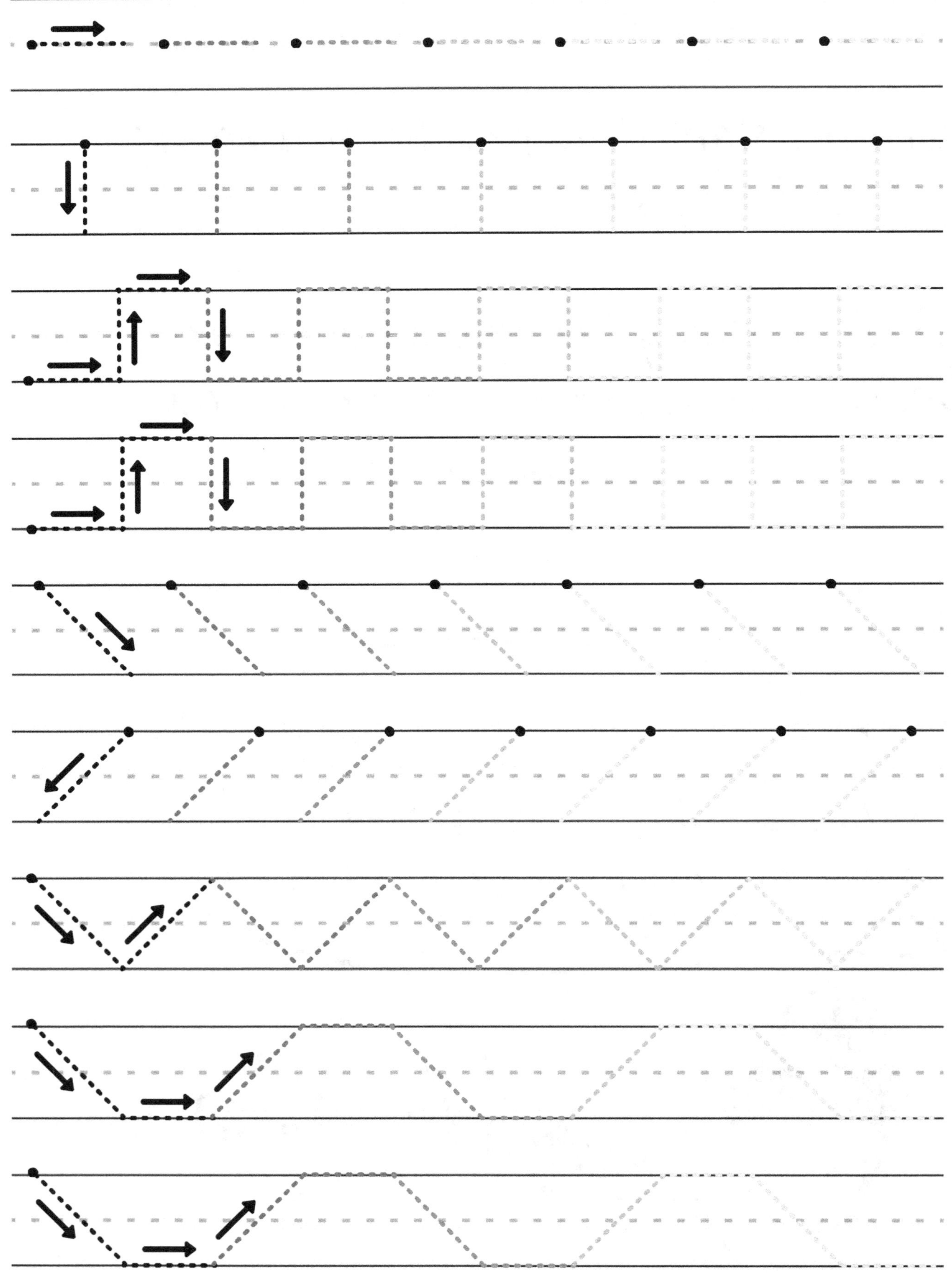

Trace the curved lines

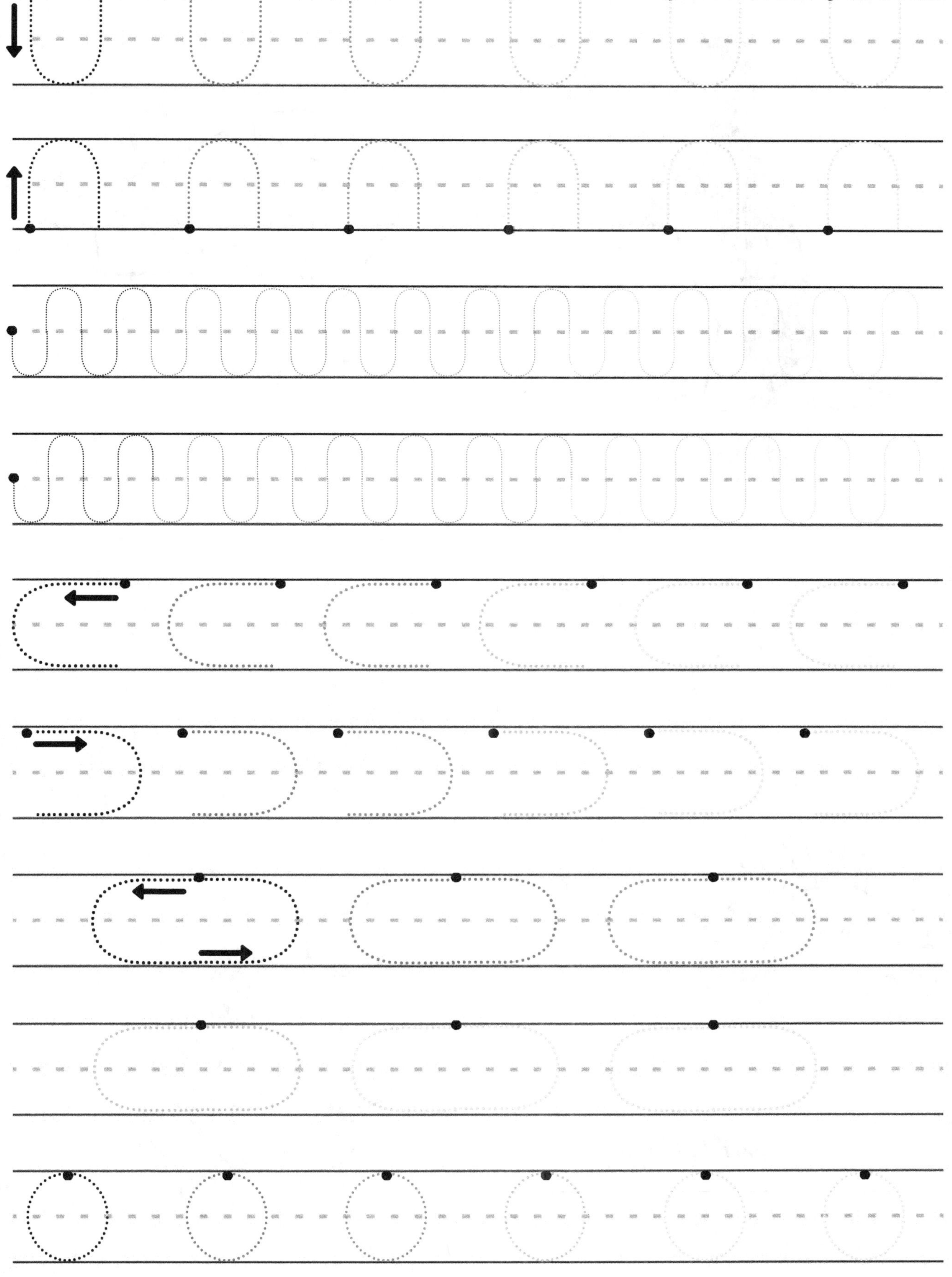

Help the otter find the urchin

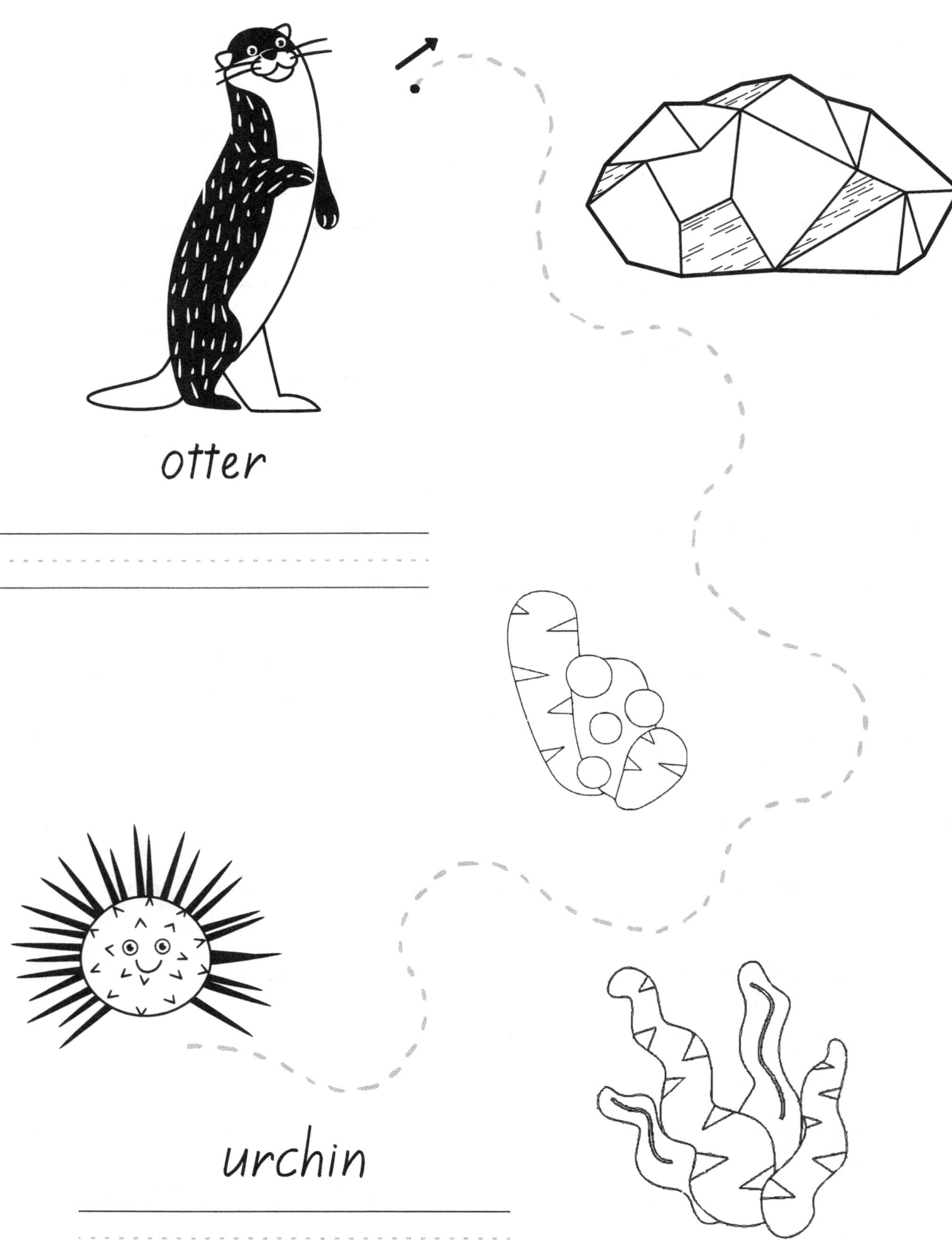

Help the bee fly to her honey

Help the alpaca go across the world to get to the zorilla

alpaca

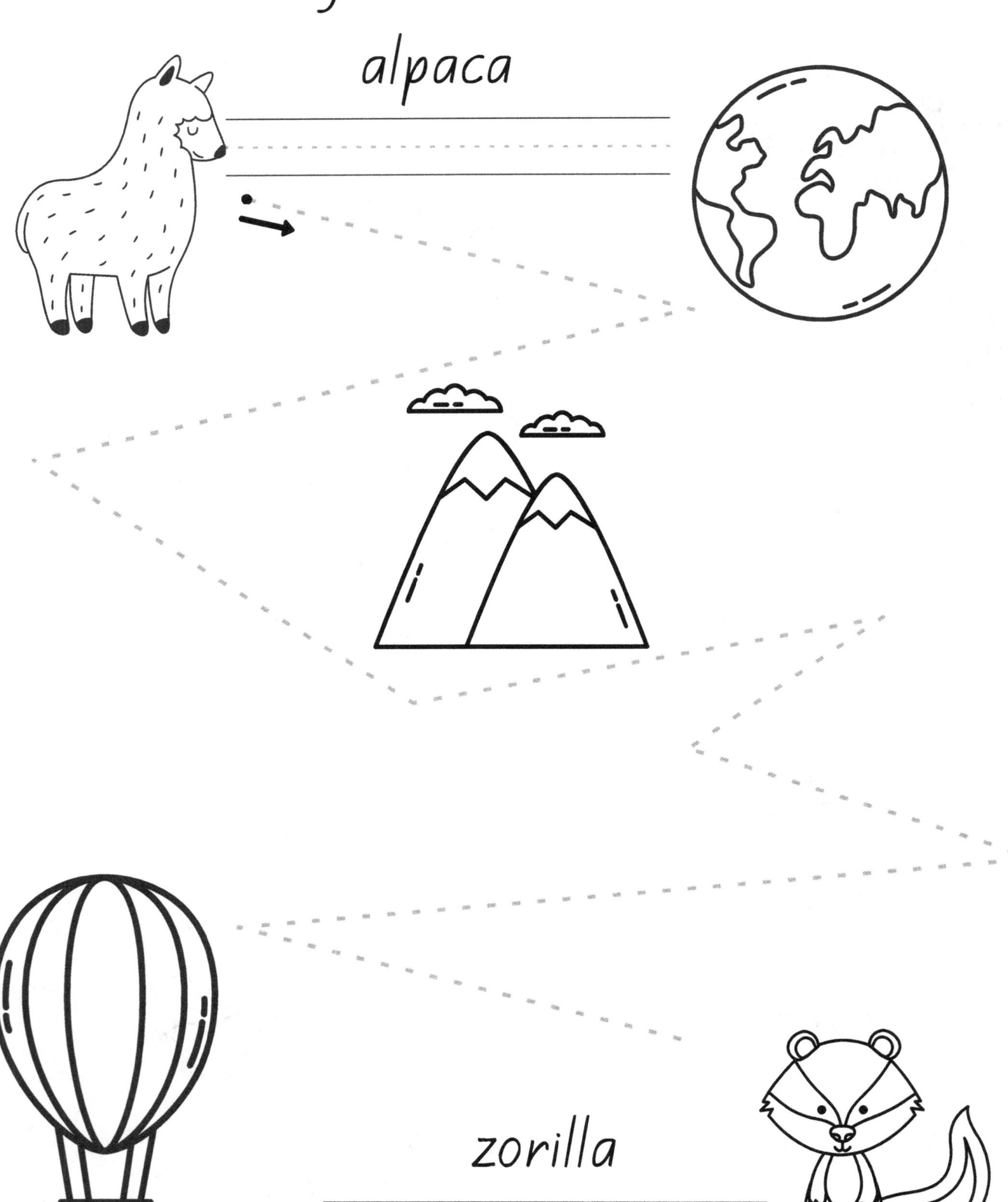

zorilla

Help the mouse get to the cheese

mouse

cheese

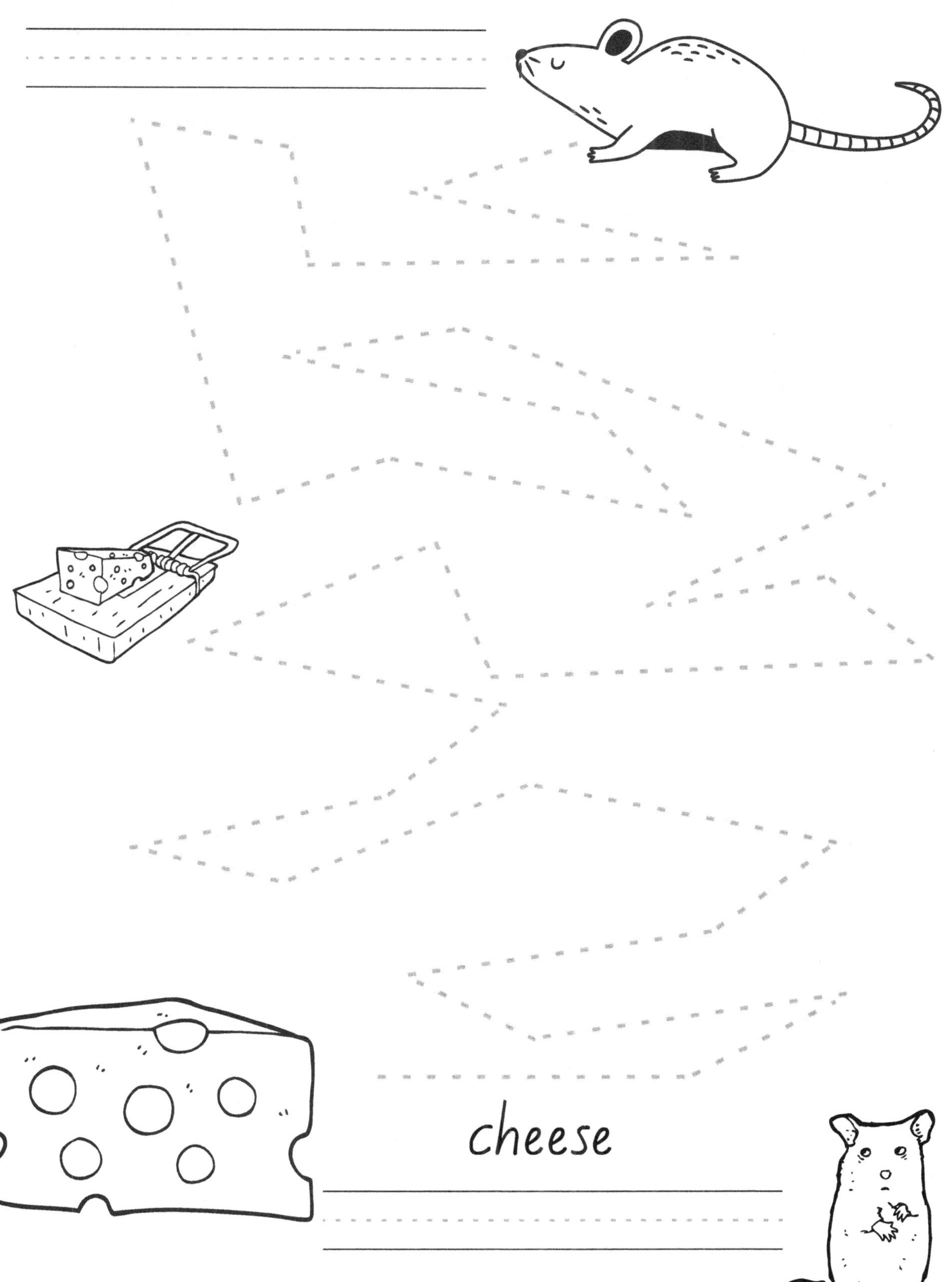

Here comes the A B C.
So much fun for you and me.
Write the letter
Color the art
Practice makes better
'Til you know it by heart.

A is for Alpaca

B b

B is for Bee

C c

C is for Crab

A B C D E F G H I J K L M N O P Q R S T U V W X Y Z

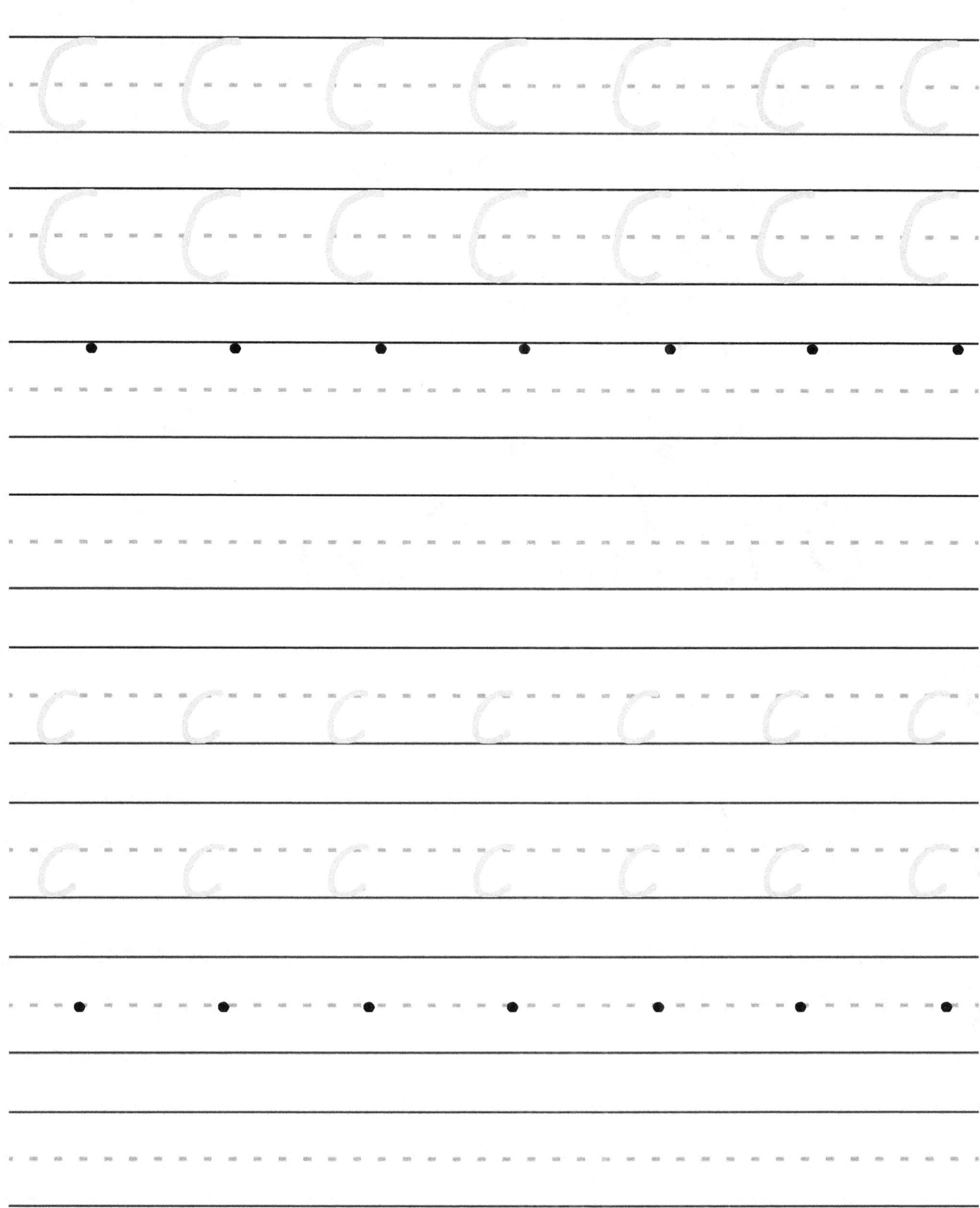

D is for Deer

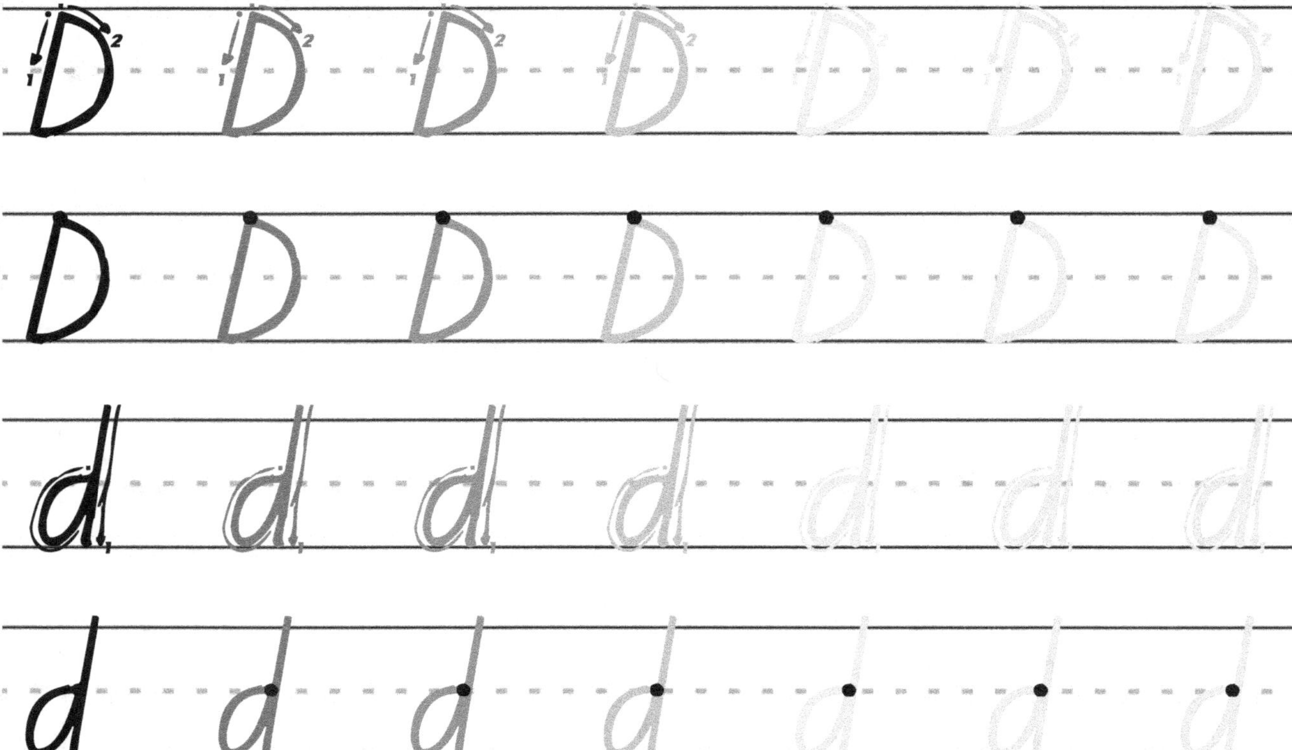

A B C D E F G H I J K L M N O P Q R S T U V W X Y Z

E e

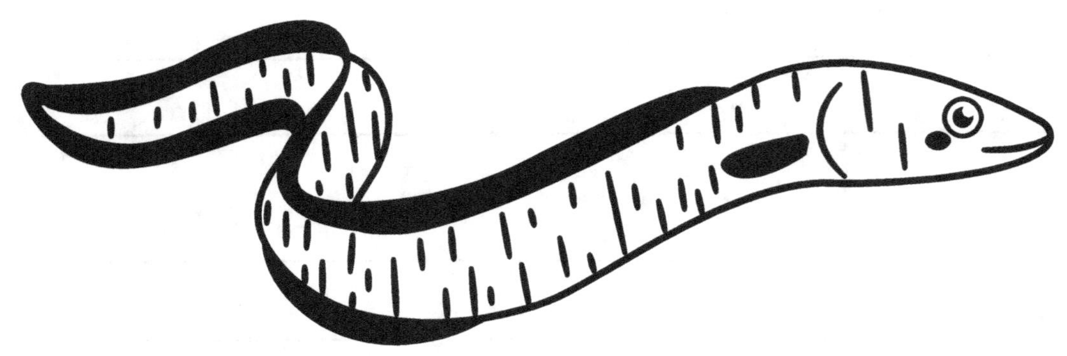

E is for Eel

A B C D E F G H I J K L M N O P Q R S T U V W X Y Z

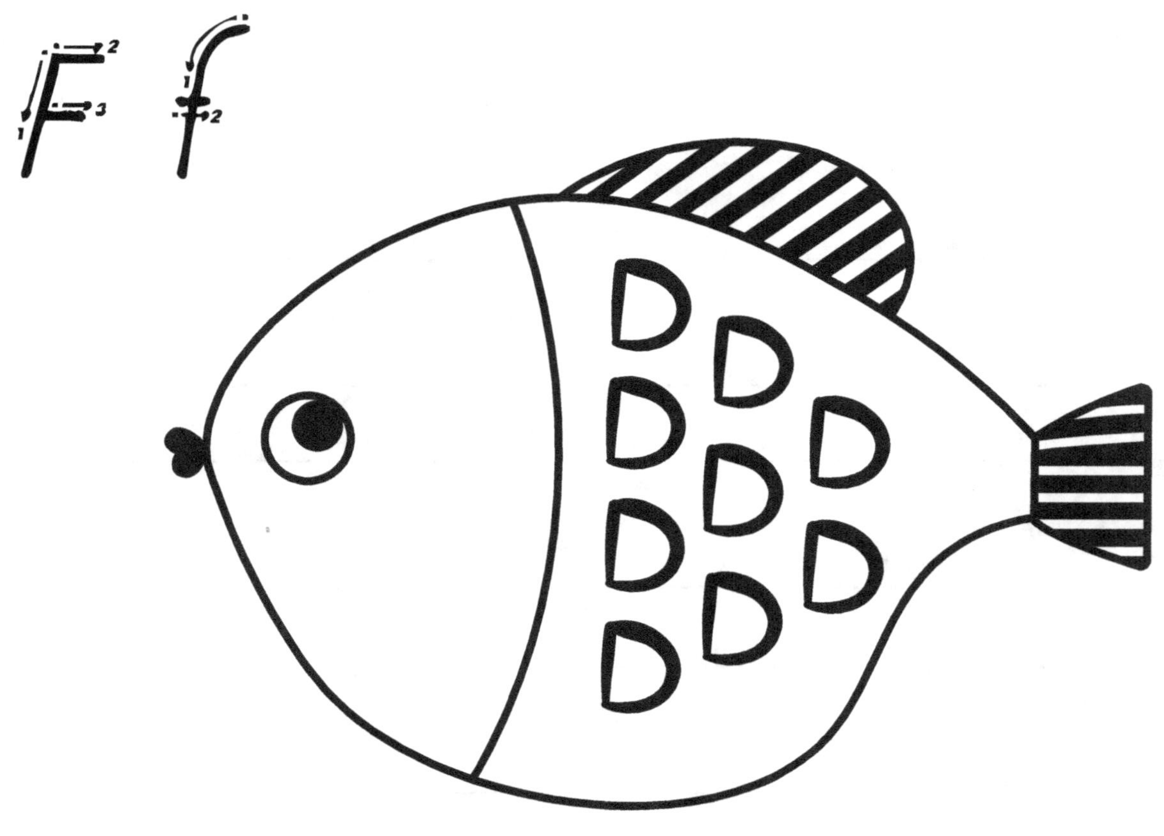

F is for Fish

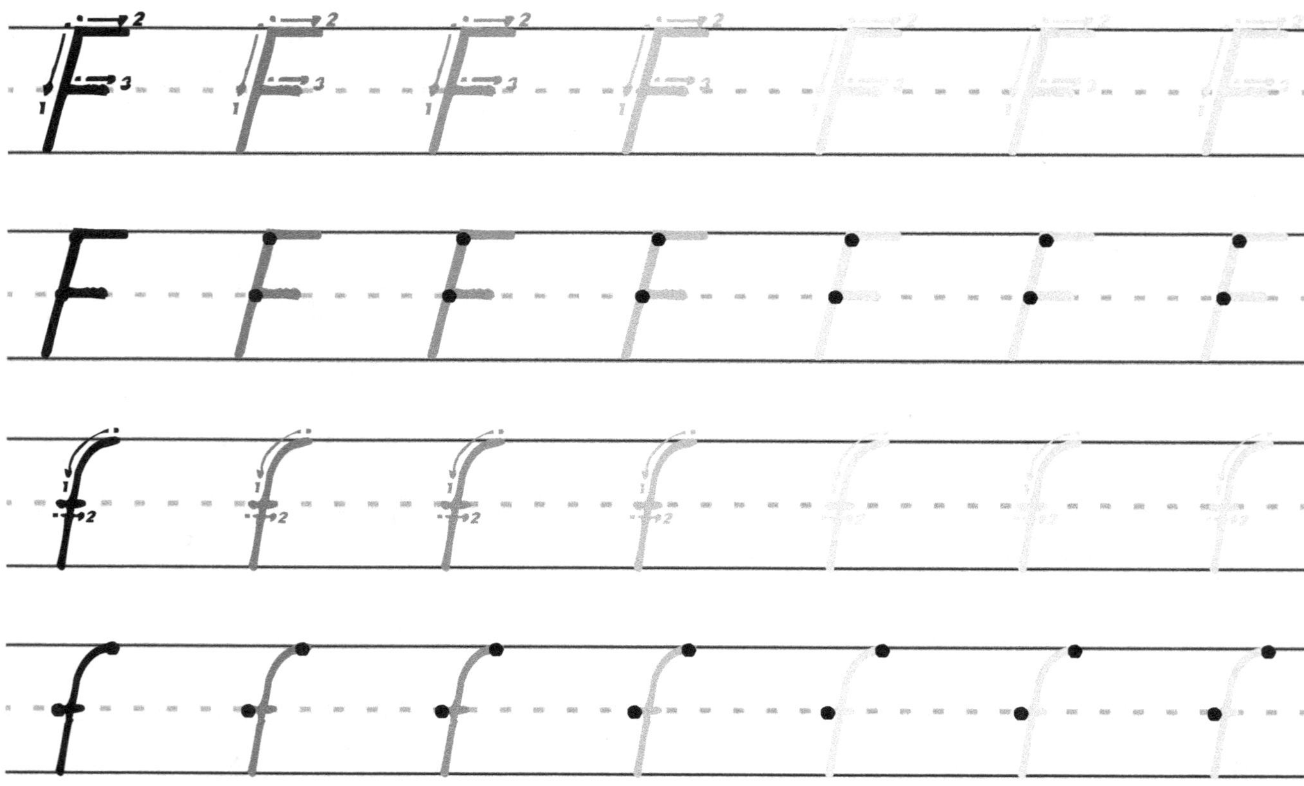

A B C D E F G H I J K L M N O P Q R S T U V W X Y Z

G g
G is for Guinea Pig

H h

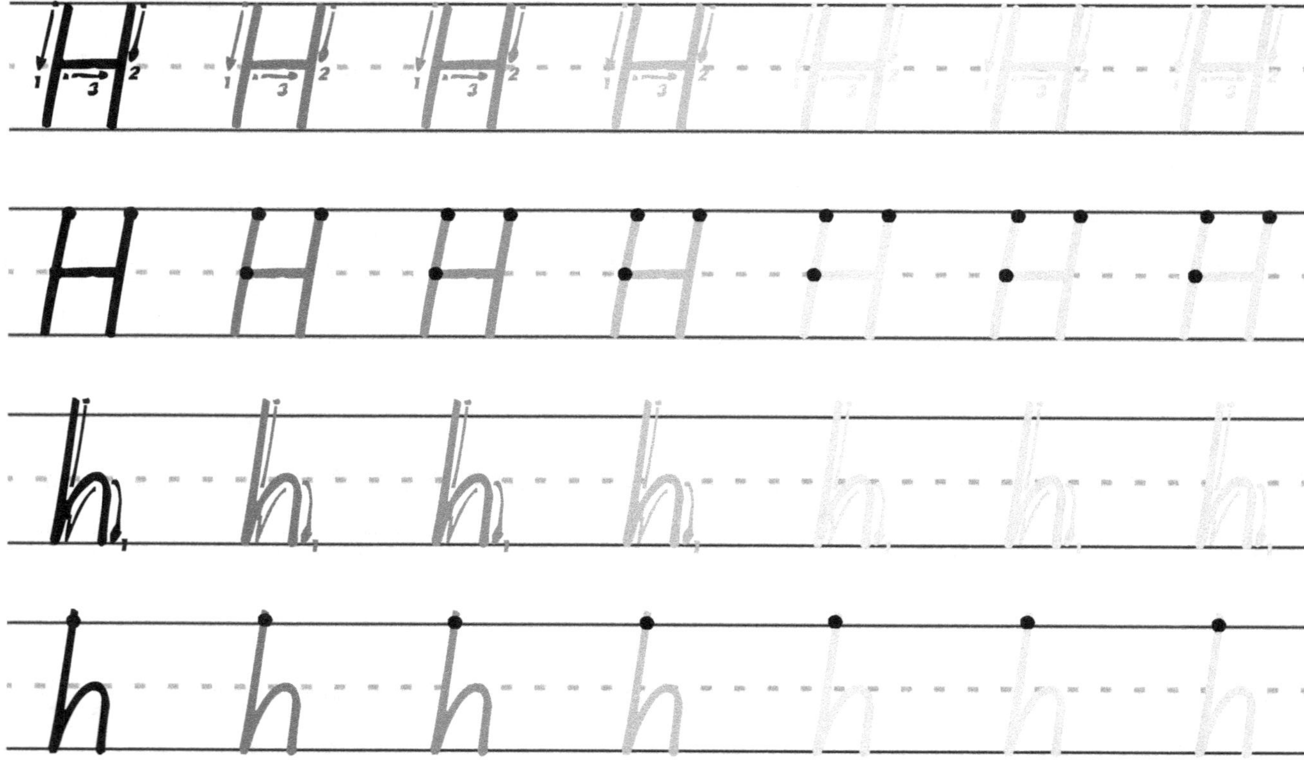

H is for Hen

A B C D E F G H I J K L M N O P Q R S T U V W X Y Z

I is for Inchworm

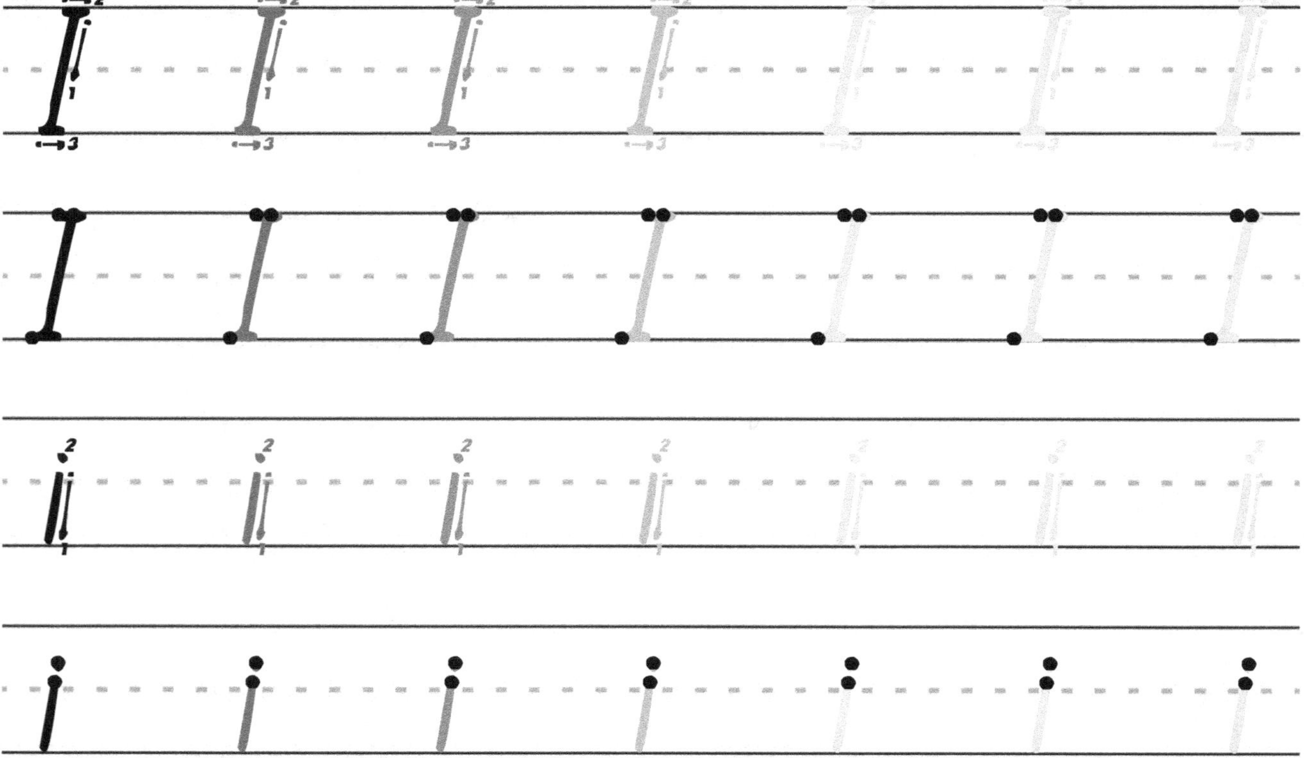

J is for Jellyfish

K k

K is for Kiwi

L is for Llama

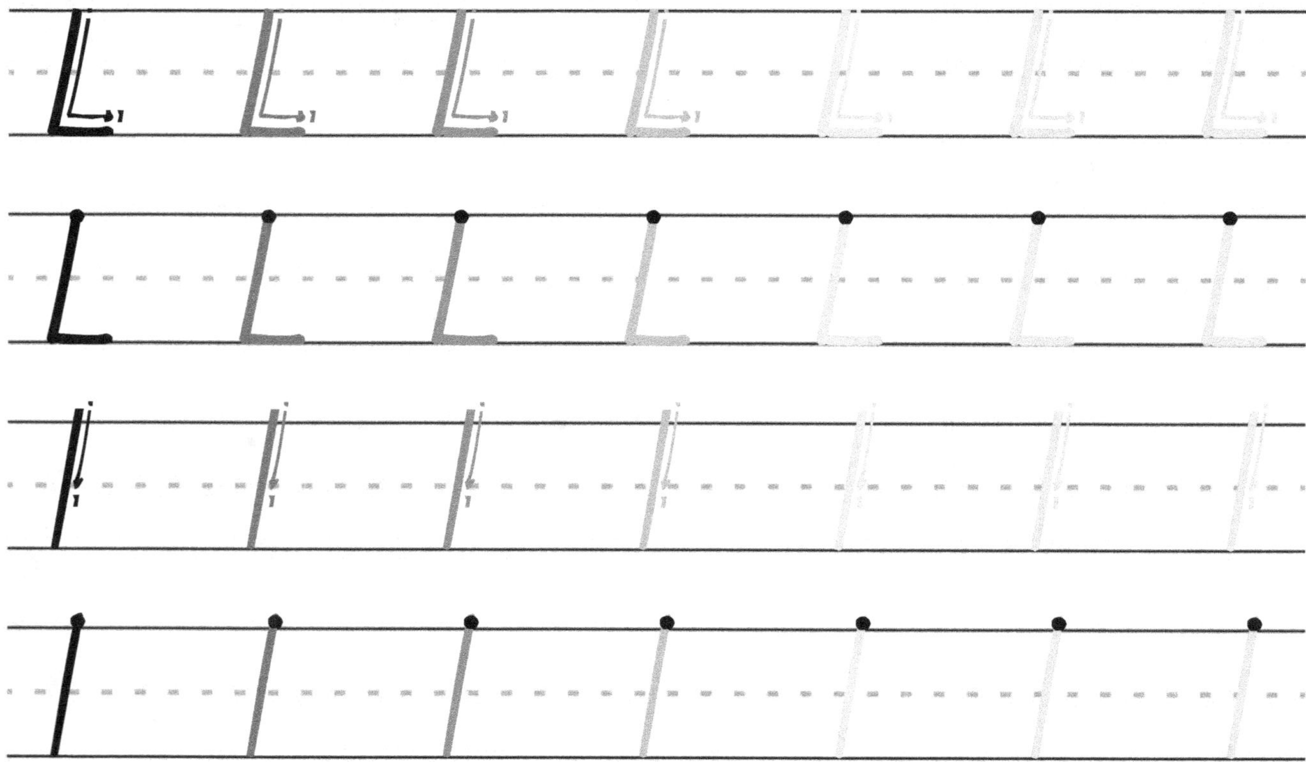

M m

M is for Mouse

ABCDEFGHIJKL M NOPQRSTUVWXYZ

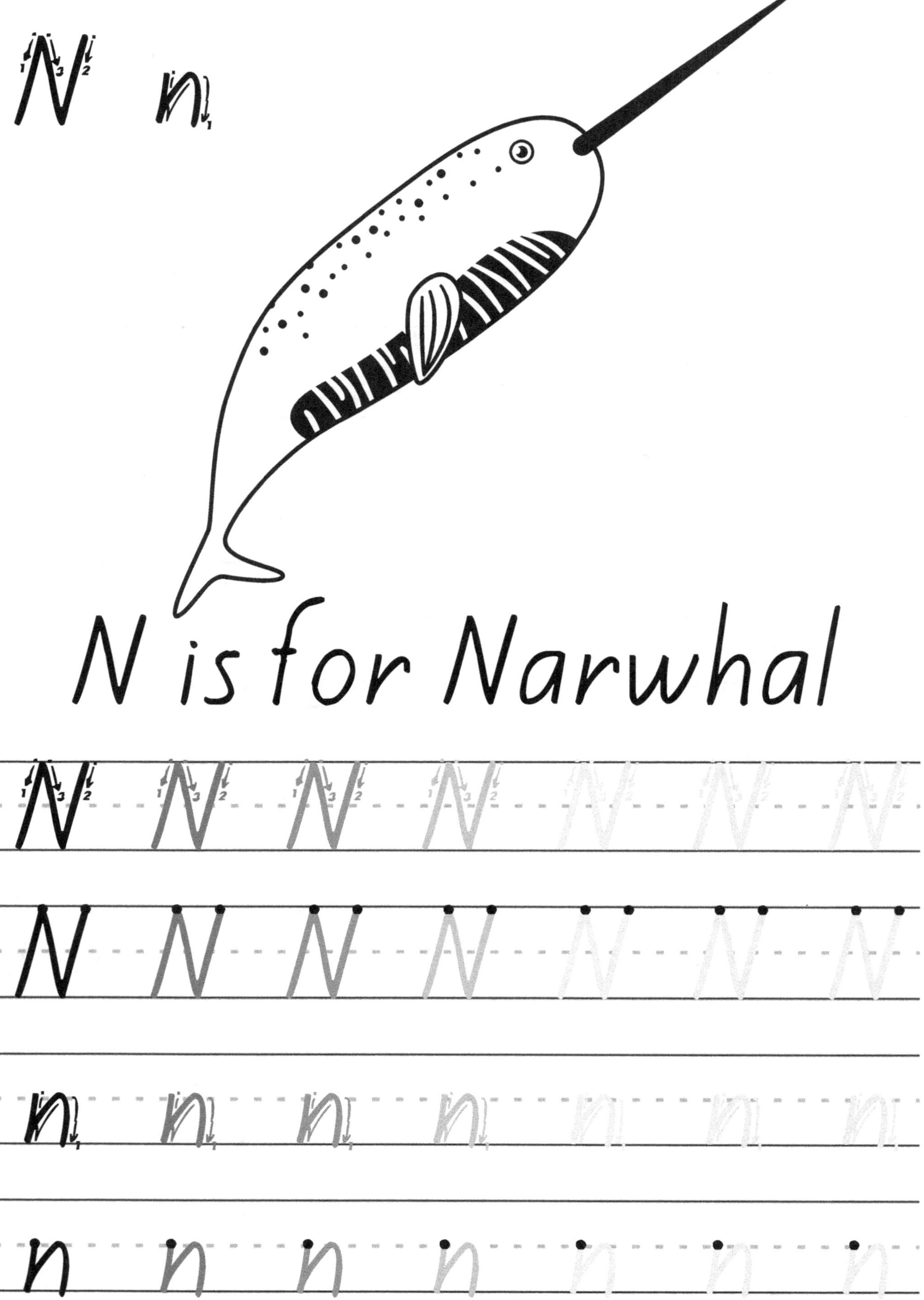

N is for Narwhal

O is for Ox

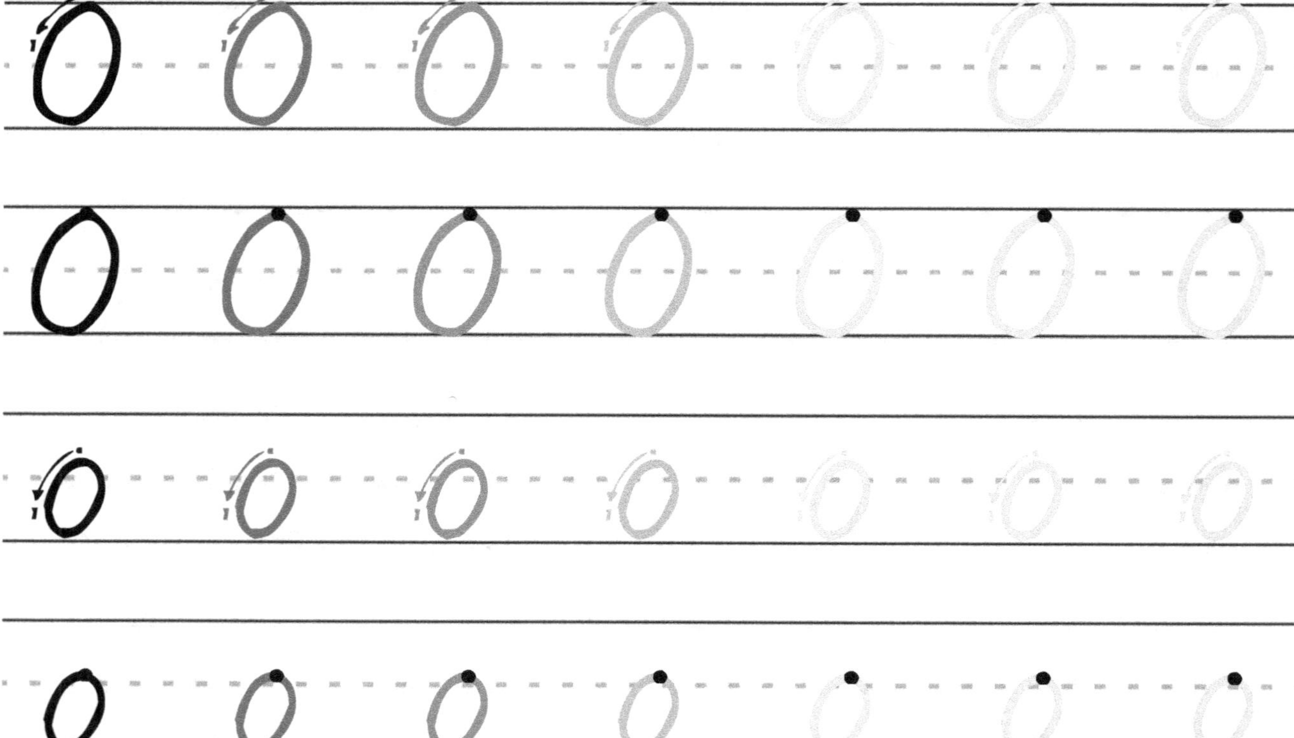

P is for Pigeon

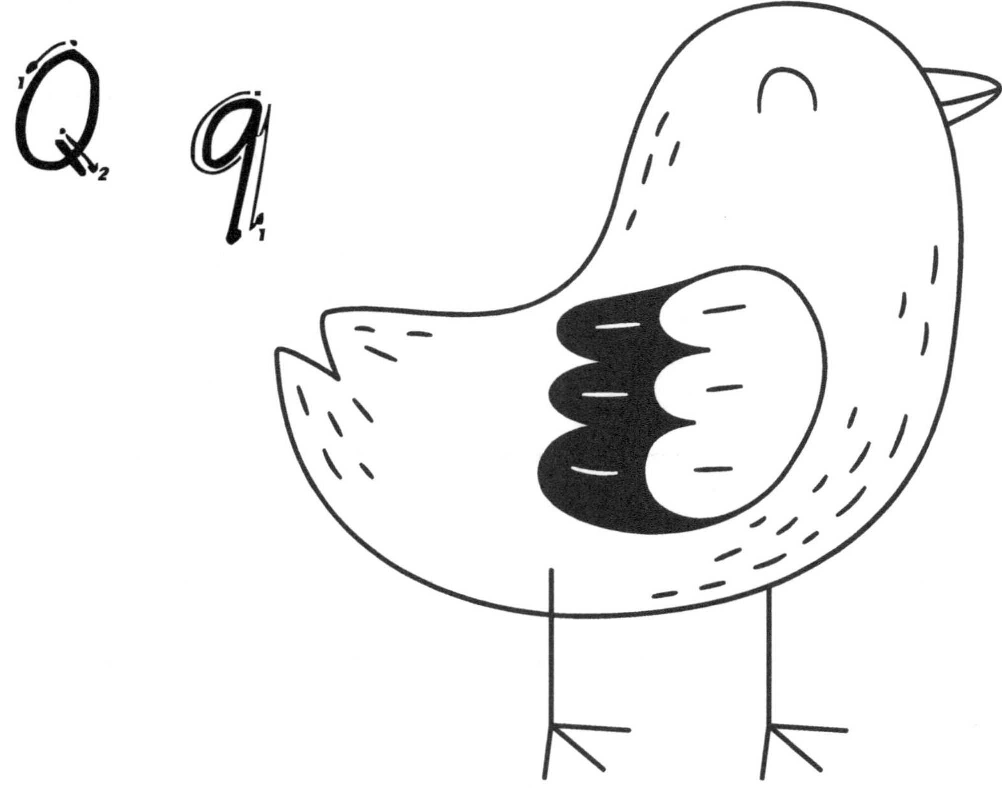

Q is for Quelea

A B C D E F G H I J K L M N O P Q R S T U V W X Y Z

R r

R is for Rooster

A B C D E F G H I J K L M N O P Q R S T U V W X Y Z

S s

S is for Stingray

A B C D E F G H I J K L M N O P Q R S T U V W X Y Z

T is for Turkey

A B C D E F G H I J K L M N O P Q R S T U V W X Y Z

U is for Urchin

A B C D E F G H I J K L M N O P Q R S T U V W X Y Z

V is for Viper

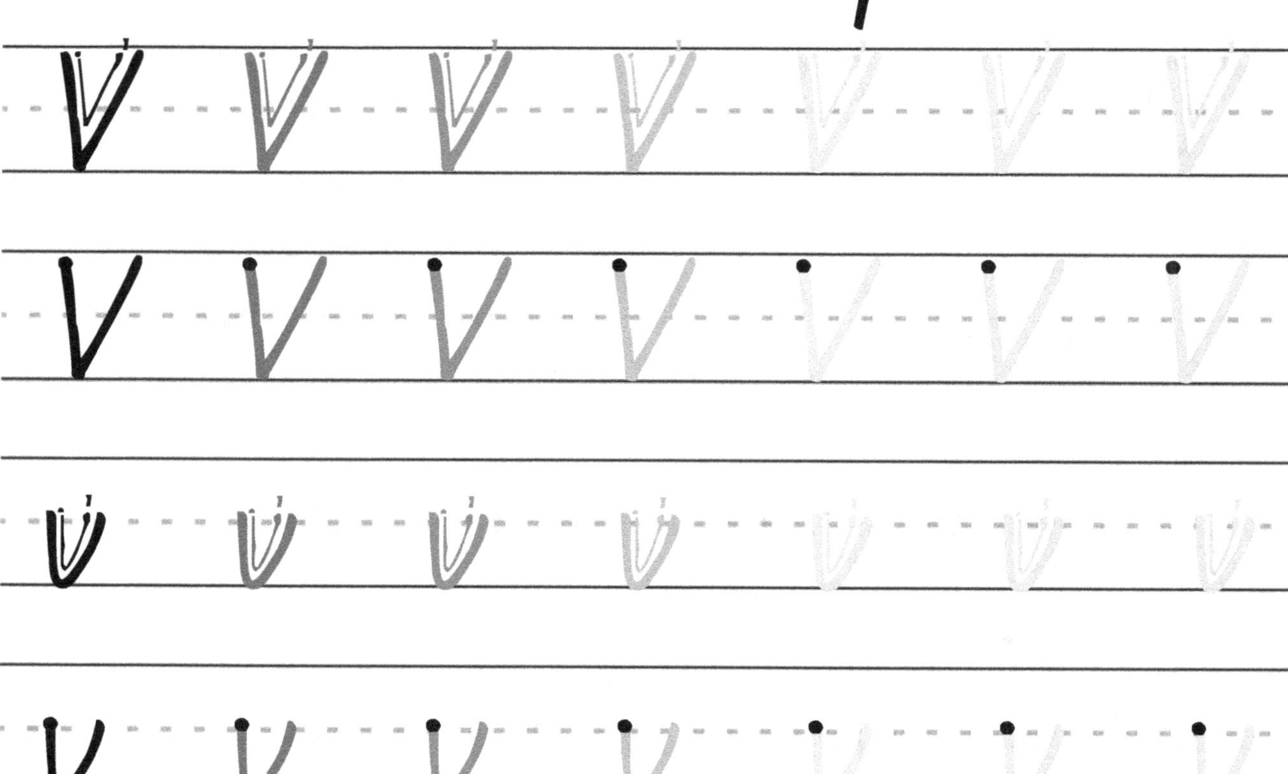

A B C D E F G H I J K L M N O P Q R S T U V W X Y Z

W is for Walrus

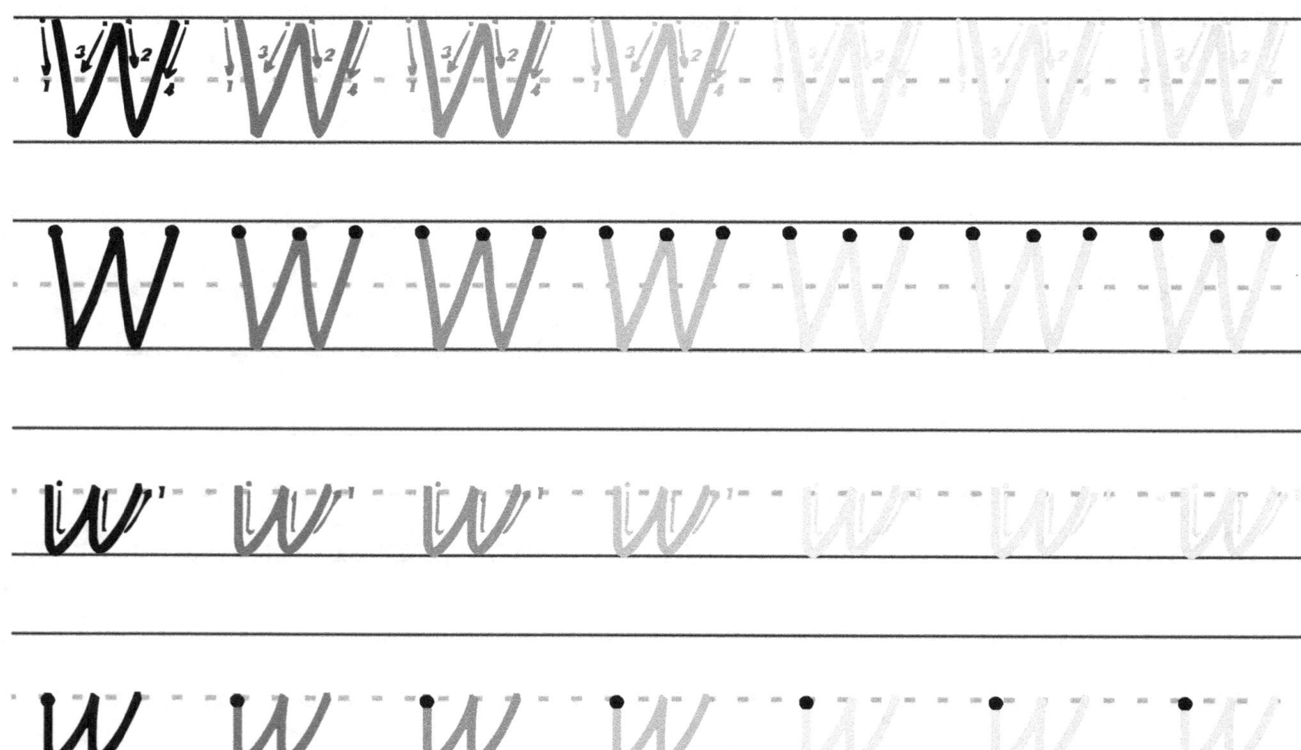

X is for Xerus

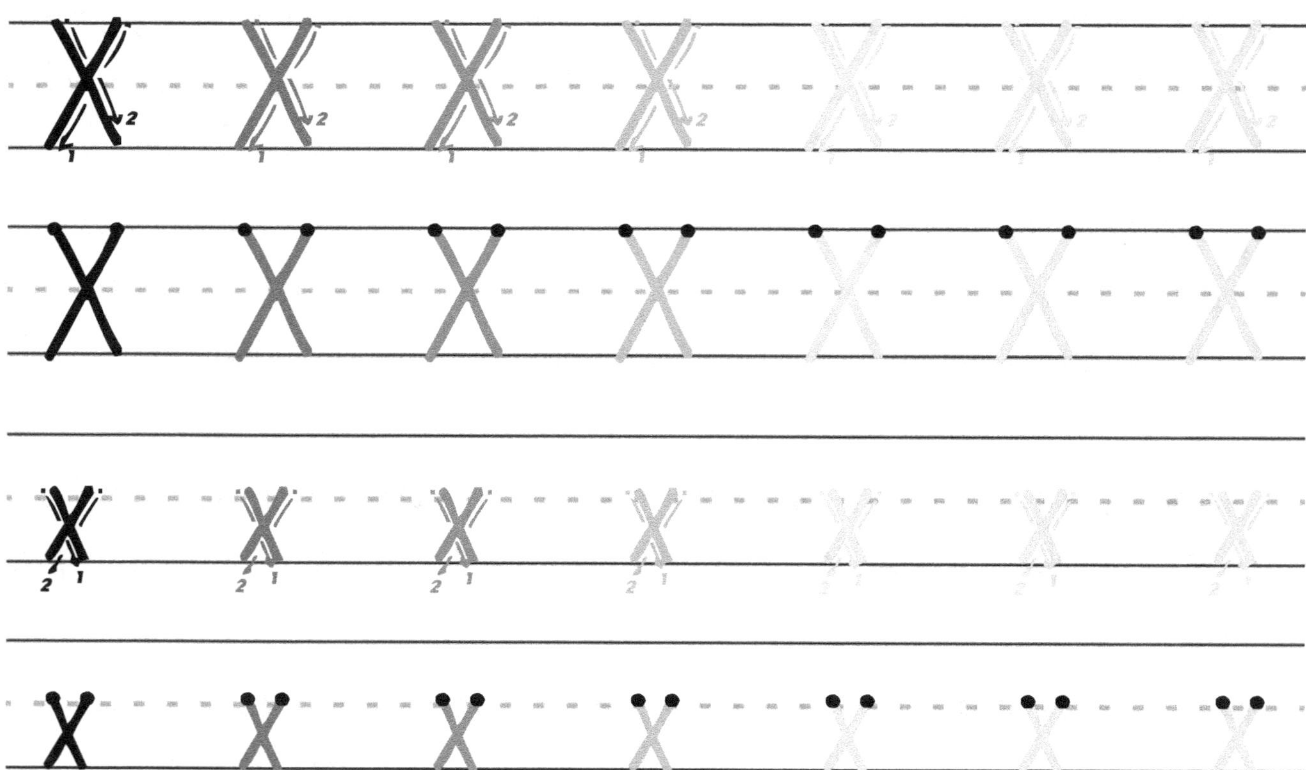

Y y

Y is for Yak

Z z

Z is for Zorilla

You did it. Now you can practice writing WORDS. Aaand... lots of coloring ahead.

Circle all the animals that contain the letter "i"

squid

swordfish

reindeer

goat

duck

pig

turtle

donkey

Circle all animals that start with the letter "s"

horse

sheep

seahorse

octopus

cow

sea lion

starfish

llama

Circle all animals that end with the letter "t"

hermit crab

lobster

rabbit

cat

seal

buffalo

dolphin

pigeon

Circle all animals that contain the letter "l"

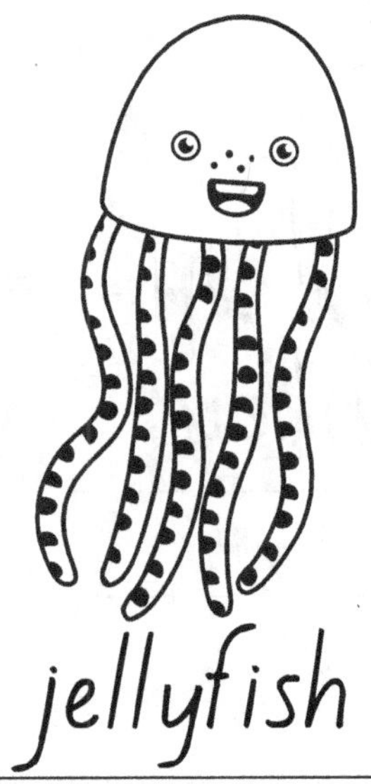

jellyfish

cuttlefish

penguin

puffer fish

silkworm

carabao

shark

mouse

Circle all animals that contain the letter "o"

otter

ox

donkey

crab

goose

stingray

clownfish

yak

Circle all animals that contain the letter "c"

alpaca

dog

salmon

whale

walrus

hen

mackerel

narwhal

Circle all animals that contain the letter "n"

gold fish

fowl

flounder

guinea pig

deer

orca

eel

lionfish

Circle all animals that contain the letter "k"

manta ray

tilapia

turkey

flowerhorn

rooster

urchin

bee

quelea

You're a pro now.
It's time to
write sentences.

this is an excited star fish

the rabbit is happy

the sea horse is looking
for his friend, the crab

the sheep is sleepy

horses run fast

the puffer fish is toxic 

the hen and the rooster

are both chickens

carabaos are strong

otters eat urchins

the eel likes to swim

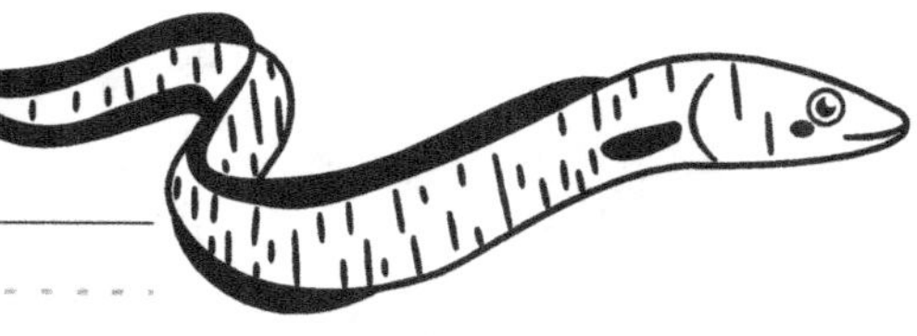

flounders have both eyes
on one side of their head

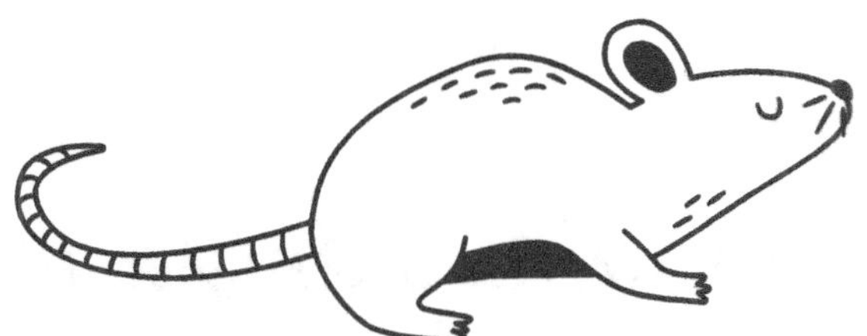

the mouse sees the pig

cats and dogs are pets

the alpaca and the llama
look alike

the crab walks sideways

seahorses have no teeth

this hermit crab says HI

the quelea likes to have
a lot of friends

this is a stubborn donkey

female goats make milk

lion fish are dangerous

this walrus loves to

sleep on the beach

CONGRATULATIONS
You've made it.
It's party time.

Certificate of

COMPLETION

awarded to

____

for successful completion of the "Letter Tracing & Coloring Book" on

____